Making Love for Him:

A Book Intended to Enlighten and Inspire Men

In Their Relationships with Women

And to Raise Their Aspirations

As to What They Might Attain

By

Mary L. Seager, MS, LPC

Dedication

_____

I dedicate this book to all the men in my life whose shining examples have inspired it, to my husband, whose brilliant ideas first gave it conception, and to my Father in Heaven, whose guiding hand I acknowledge in every word of it. I thank you all.

—Mary Seager

Contents

Foreword

Making Love for Him is a book intended to enlighten and inspire men in their relationships with women and to raise their aspirations as to what they might attain. This book is based upon the premise that *Making Love for Him* is not necessarily all about planning specific strategies to get *her* into bed, though sexual impulses are often what motivate him. Testosterone is a powerful tool, and we ought to thank God for it. How else would our species have survived for so long? How could any species have survived without it? Some *body* or some *thing* has to get the ball rolling, and it usually is the male who takes the initiative to engage in physical aspects of romance regardless of what species he belongs to. More than a few men and women would disagree with that premise in regard to their own personal relationships and as pertaining to certain societal and species-specific exceptions. However, as a general rule, man tends to be the pursuer, and aggression belongs to the male. Take a look at what we're equipped with. *It's the pestle that grinds against the mortar, not the other way around.*

So, getting back to the premise that men fundamentally want more in their relationships with women than just pursuing a sexual release, what other factors might be considered to motivate *him* in his interactions with *her?* According to Carl Rogers,[1] one of the great interpersonal

---

[1] Rogers, C. R. (1961). *On Becoming a Person: A Therapist's View of Psychotherapy.* Boston, MA: Houghton Mifflin Company.

theorists of all time, men attempt to fulfill three fundamental needs. First, they strive to be loved and respected. Second, they hope to find acceptance, and, third, they seek for mutual understanding. Love is not necessarily a given in a relationship. More often than not, it has to be earned, and a certain amount of learning and effort may be required of a man in his pursuit of a woman's *love and respect*. Her *acceptance* of him is most assuredly within her own power to give or deny as she chooses, and he may or may not be able to influence that. However, as in the case with love, enhanced knowledge and endeavor on his part may promote her reception of him as he stands before her in all his glory and with all his differences and similarities proudly on display. Mutual *understanding* comes about as a result of practiced communication between people and the meanings which they hold in common based on shared experience. So, in regard to man's pursuit of woman, how does he gain her love and respect, wherein might he find her acceptance, and what effort is required that he and she might come to understand one another as they walk their separate walks but dance their common dance of life? Contained within the chapters that follow are some simple *but meaningful* ideas intended to answer those essential questions.

In addition *and of equal importance* is man's ability to establish permanence in his relationship once he has gained the object of his desire. *How significant is it for him to climb to the top of the tallest snowy mountain if all he can do is long for scorching deserts once he has arrived?* So, too, in relationships, man must be resolute in pursuing to fruition those goals upon which he has set his sights, in loving to the very end the woman his pursuits have won him, and in being unto her all that was promised on bended knee. In being true unto her, he is being true to himself, and remaining stable and steadfast over time is the greatest test of his character. In developing such longevity, it is necessary for a man to hone certain personal attributes, to find within his relationship a mutually comfortable degree of interconnectedness, and to acquire the ability to help resolve problems that may arise over time. Those aspects of *his* alliance with *her* will also be a focus of the treatise that follows.

Part One

"To Have . . .

Chapter One

"Chivalry is Not Dead."

———————

Men want to be loved and respected by women. They want to be held in positions of honor in the lives of those whom they cherish. They want to be kings in their own castles. Hence, "chivalry is not dead,"[2] *or at least it shouldn't be*, not if men want to achieve what they most hope for. Webster's Dictionary[3] defines *chivalry* as

> the medieval institution of knighthood as bound by a special code of honor and duty; the position, character, spirit, or virtues proper to a knight, as valor, magnanimity, courtesy, or helpfulness; noble gallantry; knights collectively; hence, gallant warriors or gentlemen.

Whether men know it or not, chivalry is a meaningful concept that contains many ingredients pertinent to

———————

[2] It is apparently an anonymous individual who was responsible for first coining that phrase. Edmund Burke (1729-1797) is quoted as saying, "The age of chivalry is gone." Sir Thomas Malory (ca. 1405-1471) wrote of chivalry as being the code of conduct exemplified by King Arthur and the Knights of the Round Table in his literary masterpiece, *Le Morte d'Arthur*, a work that was completed less than 2 years before his death.

[3] Kellerman, D. F. (1975). *New Webster's Dictionary of the English Language* (College Ed.). New York, NY: Delair Publishing Company, Inc. The reader is referred to this citation for all subsequent mention of Webster.

developing and maintaining successful relationships with women. Perhaps, by breaking that idea into its component parts, we might gain a better awareness of what chivalry really is and how it can be applied in our lives and in our love relationships.

"To Hold in Honor"

Among the defining words Webster used to explain chivalry, *honor* is the first that might be considered filled with significance in regard to relationships. It is thought to be "an exemplary sense of personal moral standards and conduct" and "chastity or purity in a woman." It also means "to hold in honor or high respect; to show respect to; treat with honor; to confer honor or distinction upon; to accept and pay when due, as a bill; to carry out or fulfill, as a promise." Simply stated, honor in a man's relationship with a woman means that he abides by the things he believes in and does what he says he's going to do. It denotes being honest with himself and his partner and treating others as he would hope to be treated. It means having integrity and being true.

One can speak of an illusive ideal such as honor, but it is only by observing it in action and applying it in one's own life that it takes on true meaning and significance. I am pleased to say that I have observed and experienced within my own family and immediate acquaintance examples of honor that instill within me a true knowledge of its meaning and how very important it is. My own father reportedly honored his belief of maintaining virtue and chastity in his dating relationships, and he and my mother waited to consummate their affection towards one another until after their marriage. My father was very attractive to

4

members of the opposite sex and was known for being the most handsome man on his college campus, *as shared with me by one of his former classmates, a female,* when he met my mother, his junior of 8 years. According to his own account, despite having engaged in the opportunity to date approximately a hundred women during his years as a bachelor, he held fast to a code of moral purity and honor. During his bachelorhood, he served in the military and traveled as a member of a dance band. It may have seemed only natural to many men to have partaken more fully of the *physical benefits* that were likely available and even offered to him. However, by being true to those things which he believed in, he showed great integrity and strength of character and allowed those women with whom he interacted to maintain their honor and dignity as well.

Not every man believes as my father did or would hold to the same code of conduct. However, I would encourage each man to consider those things which he holds dear and to strive to act accordingly. Following are a number of questions that each man reading this book might consider in evaluating the degree to which honor holds a place in his life as well as the benefits of developing and maintaining honor in his relationships.

In considering some of your own observations and life experiences, what examples of honor in men's relationships with women come to mind? Those may include, but are not limited to, interactions between parents, grandparents, uncles and aunts, neighbors, and friends.

_____

_____

_____

_____

_____

_____

_____

How do you, as a man, apply honor in your life and in your interactions with the women you know?

_____

_____

_____

_____

_____

_____

_____

_____

In what ways do you perceive you might improve?

_____

_____

_____

_____

_____

_____

_____

_____

_____

How might those improvements enhance your life and your relationships?

_____

_____

_____

_____

_____

_____

_____

_____

_____

"To Do My Duty"

The next defining word applied by Webster to the concept of chivalry is duty. The Boy Scouts of America have a motto that begins as follows: "On my honor, I'll do my best to do my duty . . ."[4] Honor has already been discussed as being that quality which drives a man to pursue to fruition that which he commits himself to do, but what is duty? According to Webster, *duty* is "that which a person is bound by any natural, moral, or legal obligation to do or perform; the obligation to do something; an act of obedience or respect, esp. respectful conduct toward one's parents or elders."

Therefore, duty, as applied to a man's relationship with a woman, is a sense of commitment, devotion, or obligation to perform those things which might naturally be expected under given conditions such as dating, engagement, marriage, and fatherhood. His conduct toward her should be no less respectful than what he might offer his parents under the best of circumstances and his willingness to follow through with her expectations in their relationship no less than what he would afford an employer in a meaningful occupation. He can only expect to get out of a situation as much as he is willing to put into it.

I've witnessed duty in action. I had the unique opportunity to observe my future husband from an objective distance for more than a year prior to actually dating him. We were both working for the same employer at that time. I was engaged in providing mental-health therapy for clients at our agency and my future husband in offering security services. What I noticed through my casual observations of him was the high degree of devotion in which he carried out his work responsibilities. He was always on duty when and where he was supposed to be and

[4] Seton, E. T. (1911). *The Boy Scouts of America: The Official Handbook for Boys*. Garden City, NY: Doubleday, Page & Company.

well invested in providing security in behalf of our employer. I was impressed with the idea that, if he could only apply that same quality in his personal relationships, he would make an outstanding life's partner, and I put my theory to the test. I've never been disappointed on that account. My husband has exceeded my greatest expectations of what I might have hoped for in a relationship. For more than a decade, whether as my dating partner, my fiancée, or my husband, he has been loyal to me and to my children and has made us the focus of his love and devotion. I only hope he's getting half as much out of our relationship as I am.

Another man who comes to mind when I consider the qualities of duty and devotion is my father. I witnessed him rising before dawn, traveling a significant distance to get to work everyday, fully investing himself on the job prior to making the long trek home, and then, primarily without complaint, lending a hand to assist my mother in preparing the evening meal and caring for the children before retiring to bed so he could start the process all over again the next day. It's no wonder I set my sights so high in looking for my own companion or that I found him because I knew what I was looking for. I'd seen it done . . . *and done to near perfection.*

Speaking of my father, he was the old-fashioned sort who opened doors for women and allowed them first entrance into buildings. He even walked closest to the road in a vestigial attempt to protect his female companion from being splattered by the mud that may have been an actual threat in horse-and-buggy days. What a gentleman he was and how important he felt it was for a woman to be a lady. How sad it is that the days of ladies and gentlemen are far gone from us and that some may even take offense at those slightly archaic ideals. Such actions are more than a kindness. They are tangible reminders of man's duty to woman, to protect and defend her, *as is his way*.

In regard to my own husband, I remember how well he performed his manly duties on our first outing together. We were searching for something on a hillside, and the footing was a bit treacherous on our way down. He offered me his hand in an effort to assist me. I extended my hand and allowed it to hover over his while I jumped the remaining feet to level ground. I was too shy to actually touch him, but I remembered his kind gesture and his sense of duty toward me as a woman. It wasn't long before I took his hand on a far more permanent basis.

In considering some of your own observations and life experiences, what examples of duty in men's relationships with women come to mind? Again, those may include, but are not limited to, interactions between parents, grandparents, uncles and aunts, neighbors, and friends.

_____

_____

_____

_____

_____

_____

_____

_____

_____

How do you, as a man, apply duty in your life and in your interactions with the women you know?

_____

_____

_____

_____

_____

_____

_____

_____

In what ways do you perceive you might improve?

_____

_____

_____

_____

_____

_____

_____

_____

_____

How might those improvements enhance your life and your relationships?

_____

_____

_____

_____

_____

_____

_____

_____

"Where the Brave Dare Not Go"[5]

Webster describes *virtue* in a variety of ways, not the least of which is an "inherent power to produce effects; potency." If one does something *by virtue of* or *in virtue of*, he is doing it "by the power, force, or authority of." It was through virtue that Lancelot raised Sir Dinadan from the

_____

[5] "The Impossible Dream (The Quest)" composed by Mitch Leigh with lyrics written by Joe Darion for the 1965 musical *Man of La Mancha*

dead,[6] a depiction reminiscent of Christ's own power and authority. Among the "virtues proper to a knight," as spoken of by Webster, *valor* is the first and is defined as "that quality which enables a man to encounter danger with firmness; personal bravery, esp. in fighting; intrepidity; prowess." The potency of valor is witnessed in a man's willingness to go "where the brave dare not," as did Don Quixote de La Mancha, who tread upon dangerous ground in entering the life of Aldonza, a forlorn and embittered woman who lashed out at him in pain. Yet, through his daring tenderness, he instilled within her the hope necessary to turn her life about.[7]

What does it mean for a man to be valiant in the life of a woman? In my estimation, it signifies his willingness to set his own safety at naught as he stands with her in times of trouble and despair. Finances, illness, family and other relationship problems, and work-related concerns all are potential triggers for words of anger or bouts of tears. A man can be somewhat of a lashing post or a shoulder to cry on as the situation and the woman's temperament may dictate. Patience and calm resolve on his part are most certainly required when emotion takes its "pound of flesh"[8] from her. His quiet presence can comfort her and instill within the hope for a brighter day ahead.

My husband has pointed out to me on more than one occasion my inclination to take my feelings out on him

---

[6] Warner, J. (Producer), & Logan, J. (Director). (1967). *Camelot* [Motion Picture]. United States: Warner Bros. Pictures - Seven Arts, Inc.
[7] Hiller, A. (Producer/Director). (1972). *Man of La Mancha* [Motion Picture]. Italy: United Artists Pictures, Inc.
[8] reference to Shakespeare's *Merchant of Venice*

when things in my own life aren't as I might hope for them to be. An argument with my daughter, disappointment or overexertion on the job, and criticism from a variety of sources, including myself, can all send me railing at him. Why do I do that? I think it's because I know he's a safe sounding board for me. He quietly listens and tries to comfort me to the best of his ability. It's only after the storm has passed that he may try to place a bit more objective perspective on things and help me to see the role I may be playing in my own demise or in the angst he may be quietly holding within. His calm assurance acts as a protective shield for both of us.

In considering some of your own observations and life experiences, what examples of valor in men's relationships with women come to mind? Again, those may include, but are not limited to, interactions between parents, grandparents, uncles and aunts, neighbors, and friends.

_____

_____

_____

_____

_____

_____

_____

_____

_____

How do you, as a man, apply valor in your life and in your interactions with the women you know?

_____

_____

_____

_____

_____

_____

_____

_____

In what ways do you perceive you might improve?

_____

_____

_____

_____

_____

_____

_____

_____

_____

How might those improvements enhance your life and your relationships?

_____

_____

_____

_____

_____

_____

_____

_____

"Noble and Great Ones" (Abraham 3:22)[9]

The second virtue "proper to a knight" is that of magnanimity. *Magnanimity* is presented as "nobility or dignity of soul or character" and *magnanimous* as "exhibiting nobleness of soul and generosity of mind; rising above ignoble motives and resentment; suggesting an elevated spirit." At the heart of magnanimity is *nobility,* or "exalted moral excellence; admirable dignity; majesty or augustness." To be *noble* is to be

of an exalted moral character or excellence; admirable in dignity of conception, or in the manner of

---

[9] Corporation of the President of the Church of Jesus Christ of Latter-Day Saints. (1981). *The Pearl of Great Price.* Salt Lake City, UT: The Church of Jesus Christ of Latter-Day Saints.

expression, execution, or composition; imposing or fine in appearance; stately or magnificent; of an admirably high quality, type, or class; fine, choice, or notably superior.

The term *noblesse* refers to "the nobility; persons of noble rank collectively" and *noblesse oblige* to "the obligation of people of wealth and social position to behave with honor and generosity; broadly, the duty to behave honorably."

In what way does magnanimity or nobility play a role in man's interactions with woman? Certainly, if she is to choose him as her life's partner, she is to look upon him as being especially fine in his physical attributes as well as his underlying character. She would be doing herself a disservice to select a companion who did not please all of her senses. His physical attractiveness spans far more than mere appearances. A woman should also love the sound of his voice, his taste and smell, and the feel of his touch on her skin. All should be in conformity *and can be* if a careful choice is made. That imposes some expectation on the male to do his very best to try to be pleasing to a woman, to attend to necessary grooming and hygiene, and to dress as attractively as his budget will allow. "Putting his best foot forward"[10] in that regard will only benefit him as he endeavors to win a woman's heart.

In regard to my own husband, I remember the first time I saw him. I had to look . . . *and look again.* His beauty amazed me. His appearances were a composite of all that I'd ever loved in a man. He was blonde, and youthful, and of a slighter build at that time. I loved the

---

[10] origin and meaning cited on www.phrases.org.uk/meanings

17

way he looked in his uniform, so crisp and professional. In growing to know him better, I noticed the thick brown hair on his forearms. Somehow, that comforted me. His scent was so appealing. The cologne he chose to wear combined with his own body chemistry to form a mild aphrodisiac. His hands were so warm and strong. Everything about him served to please me. He immediately won my heart.

In addition, the idea of noblesse oblige comes into play when magnanimity and nobility are applied to man's pursuit of woman. What he puts into the relationship will most definitely influence what he gets out of it, and heightened generosity on his part will draw her closer to him rather than push her away. One cannot place a dollar value on generosity. It is the amount a man gives in proportion to what he has that sets him apart as being truly generous. It is the time he spends, the attention and affection he devotes, and his constant observance that all her needs are met that will prove him worthy of a woman's love.

Again, my husband set himself apart from other men in that regard. From the very beginning of our relationship, he took on the role of provider in offering to pay for our excursions out together, and our meals, in addition to purchasing household items I was noticeably lacking. Knowing that his income was somewhat limited, I did not allow him to pay for everything, but I did notice his willingness to do so, and I realized his generosity exceeded that of anyone I'd known in comparison with what he had to give. That meant far more to me than fur coats or diamond rings ever could have. I'd found a winner in him, *and I wasn't about to let him go.*

In considering some of your own observations and life experiences, what examples of magnanimity and nobility in men's relationships with women come to mind? Again, those may include, but are not limited to, interactions between parents, grandparents, uncles and aunts, neighbors, and friends.

_____

_____

_____

_____

_____

_____

_____

_____

_____

How do you, as a man, apply magnanimity and nobility in your life and in your interactions with the women you know?

_____

_____

_____

_____

_____

_____

19

_____

_____

_____

In what ways do you perceive you might improve?

_____

_____

_____

_____

_____

_____

_____

_____

How might those improvements enhance your life and your relationships?

_____

_____

_____

_____

_____

"Let Us Oft Speak Kind Words" (Hymn no. 232)[11]

 Courtesy, another virtue befitting a knight, is set forth as being "politeness of manners combined with kindness; polished manners or urbanity shown in behavior toward others; an act of civility or respect; a favor or indulgence, as contradistinguished from right." I believe part of what Webster was getting at in that regard is that we all hope to be treated with kindness and respect *whether we deserve it or not* and that we all behave ourselves at times in such a manner as to engender unkindness or disrespect from others. At those moments, we all need a "knight in shining armor"[12] to come galloping up on his noble steed and patiently, forgivingly take us by the hand and lift us with words and deeds of kindness, reminding us of who we are and who we can be if only we will try a little harder.

 A man can do that for a woman. Time spent, a gentle touch, a whispered endearment, gifts and tokens of love, and helpful gestures can all sooth the embittered soul. Being treated with kindness and respect makes a woman feel loved. Feeling loved helps her to feel worthy of love. Feeling worthy of love lifts her self-esteem and allows her to act in such a manner as to deserve love and to treat

---

[11] Corporation of the President of the Church of Jesus Christ of Latter-Day Saints. (1985). *Hymns of the Church of Jesus Christ of Latter-Day Saints.* Salt Lake City, UT: Deseret Book Company.

[12] origin and meaning cited on www.phrases.org.uk/meanings

others with kindness and respect as well. Everyone wins in that ongoing circle of love.

Kindness may very well be my most favorite quality in a man. My husband certainly stood out from other men I had known in that regard. Whenever I wondered whom I should choose to spend the remainder of my life with, I would ask myself the following questions: *"Who is it that treats you well?"* and *"How do you feel when you're with him?"* My future husband was almost constantly available when I needed him and always offered a calming reassurance that I was doing well in my life. My father served that same purpose for me prior to my pairing off with the man of my dreams and offered that same support for my daughter, as she grew up without a father of her own. She recently told me how she never felt lonely when my father was with us because he constantly attended to her and looked after her needs. That is what a man can do for a woman.

My father had grown up in a household with a mother who embraced strong religious sentiment and ideals. I believe that is where many of his values stemmed from, including his kind and caring treatment of others. He took great pleasure in recounting to his children the words from his mother's favorite church hymn (no. 223).[13] It is entitled *Have I Done Any Good?* The words read as follows:

> *Have I done any good in the world today?*
> *Have I helped anyone in need?*
> *Have I cheered up the sad and made someone feel glad?*

---

[13] *Hymns of the Church of Jesus Christ of Latter-Day Saints.*

If not, I have failed indeed.
Has anyone's burden been lighter today
Because I was willing to share?
Have the sick and the weary been helped on their way?
When they needed my help was I there?

Then wake up and do something more
Than dream of your mansion above.
Doing good is a pleasure, a joy beyond measure,
A blessing of duty and love.

There are chances for work all around just now,
Opportunities right in our way.
Do not let them pass by, saying, "Sometime I'll try,"
But go and do something today.
'Tis noble of man to work and to give;
Love's labor has merit alone.
Only he who does something helps others to live.
To God each good work will be known.

Then wake up and do something more
Than dream of your mansion above.
Doing good is a pleasure, a joy beyond measure,
A blessing of duty and love.

Those words encompass the kind and caring qualities which my father emulated in his treatment of others, including the women in his life, and are a standard for the courtesy any man can afford a woman.

In considering some of your own observations and life experiences, what examples of courtesy and kindness in men's relationships with women come to mind? Again, those may include, but are not limited to, interactions between parents, grandparents, uncles and aunts, neighbors, and friends.

_____

_____

_____

_____

_____

_____

_____

_____

How do you, as a man, apply courtesy and kindness in your life and in your interactions with the women you know?

_____

_____

_____

_____

_____

_____

_____

_____

In what ways do you perceive you might improve?

_____

_____

_____

_____

_____

_____

_____

_____

_____

How might those improvements enhance your life and your relationships?

_____

_____

_____

_____

_____

_____

_____

_____

_____

Helpfulness is also considered to be a knightly characteristic, the quality of which is explained as being "beneficial; useful; rendering aid." In regard to helpfulness, the Boy Scouts of America once again come to mind, as they are noted for the degree to which they seek to serve others. Images of boy scouts' assisting elderly citizens across the street and soothing crying infants emerge in regard to the service they have historically offered. Speaking of *service*, a word which seems most synonymous with being helpful, many would consider Christ to be the one who gave of Himself most fully in the service of others. He gave His life for us and laid it at His Father's feet.

How does service come into play in respect to a man's interactions with a woman? How does he serve her? Can we count the ways? He is her advisor, her supporter, her loyal friend. He loves her, teaches her, meets her every need, and stands beside her in fulfilling mutual life responsibilities. He gives of his time, his talents, even of his body in the procreation of life. In nowise can he fail if he truly seeks to help her.

My father found ways of reaching out to others in an effort to be of assistance to them. As I mentioned earlier in the chapter, he was always on hand to aid my mother in preparing the evening meal. More often than not, he may have been the only one engaged in meal preparation. That was his way of showing love. I believe he learned that from his maternal grandmother and a maternal aunt. In their homes, there was always warmth, and love, *and food*, and my father often spoke affectionately of his memories of them. He offered tribute to them in establishing within his own home that same feeling of warmth and love and in preparing to the best of his ability some of the foods he had relished as he was growing up and some that had pleased his tastes when he was a young man living away from home.

I was a single mother for quite a few years before meeting my wonderful husband, and my daughter and I always enjoyed being invited to join my father and other members of my family as we gathered to eat the food that was prepared. One of our favorites was the Italian spaghetti Dad made from a recipe he procured from an Italian immigrant during his days in the military. We also loved his meatloaf, his oven-fried chicken, his Spanish-carrot stew, Swiss steak, and the frikadellers he learned to make from his Danish relatives. Food meant love to him. Preparing it and offering it to others, including my ailing maternal grandmother, were means of showing love through service. He set a great precedent for his children, and I hope I'm following in his footsteps. I'm also thankful that my husband cooks . . . *and that he does it so very well.* He has introduced me and my daughter to some wonderful meals of well-seasoned venison, beef steaks, and a variety of roasts, as well as fried chicken, oven-roasted potatoes, and lo mein.

A man does well in learning to assist in carrying out the responsibilities that have traditionally been placed upon women. A man's ability to cook, clean, wash dishes, do laundry, care for children, and shop for groceries is a plus in a woman's eyes. It is an indication that she will not be so heavily burdened to bear up under household duties on her own, as she, like her husband, may endeavor to work outside the household in addition to being a wife and mother. A man who can perform in those ways is a highly valued commodity and may win more hearts than Casanova[14] ever dreamed of.

I have a sister-in-law who mentioned that my brother does most of the cooking in their household and that she does most of the cleaning. That particular division of labor seems fairly common among our family. I believe it is part of the heritage we gained from growing up with a culinary father. Both of my older brothers are good cooks, and, as I mentioned before, so is my husband. That sharing of work responsibilities within the household engenders feelings of mutual support and love that are necessary for a meaningful and long-lasting relationship.

In considering some of your own observations and life experiences, what examples of helpfulness and service in men's relationships with women come to mind? Again, those may include, but are not limited to, interactions between parents, grandparents, uncles and aunts, neighbors, and friends.

_____

_____

_____

_____

_____

_____

[14] a famous womanizer known for the art of seduction

28

_____

_____

_____

How do you, as a man, apply helpfulness and service in your life and in your interactions with the women you know?

_____

_____

_____

_____

_____

_____

_____

_____

In what ways do you perceive you might improve?

_____

_____

_____

_____

_____

_____

_____

_____

_____

How might those improvements enhance your life and your relationships?

_____

_____

_____

_____

_____

_____

_____

_____

_____

Marching into the Workplace

The final characteristic employed by Webster to define chivalry is that of gallantry. *Gallantry* is described as the inclination to be "brave, high-spirited, or chivalrous; as, a *gallant* soldier; polite and attentive to women; courtly; flamboyantly amorous; splendid or fine; stately." In my own estimation, I believe it is gallant for a man to do those things that are characteristically male and to do so with enthusiasm and without complaint. Foremost among those is his ability to gallantly march into the workplace and earn a living well suited to his lifestyle and that of his lady. I am not saying that she does not do the same. I am merely indicating that he must take the lead in that endeavor if she is to see him as her hero, the one she follows into the forests of life.

The men I have known, my grandfathers, my father, my uncles, my brothers, and my husband, have all taken their work responsibilities seriously and have applied themselves to do their very best to fulfill their commitments in the workplace in the service of those who remain at home, their wives and children. It is not just the act of providing, but the spirit in which duties are carried out, that sets a man apart from his fellows as being a truly gallant soldier. As I have noted, enthusiasm and lack of complaint are those qualities which endear *him* to *her*.

Both of my grandfathers endeavored to earn a living for their families during the Great Depression. My father's family seemed to have been hit a bit harder by the economic struggles of the time, and my paternal grandfather, a railroad worker, had to relocate a fair distance from home and family in an effort to continue to provide support. My mother's family, on the other hand, maintained some financial stability due to the nature of my maternal grandfather's occupation as a manager of a mill. Both men, however, put forth their best efforts to support their families during those times of great financial difficulty.

As I mentioned earlier, my own father had to travel some distance to get to work everyday. As a result, his days began very early, and his nights ended very late. Though he was trained as a geologist, the job that he managed to procure was in the civil-engineering department at a military base. It was not the work that he loved to do, but it was what he had to do in order to support his family. He devoted years of service at his workplace and put forth a gallant effort in meeting his family's needs. My older brothers have both followed in our father's footsteps in traveling great distances between home and work and in meeting the needs of their families through their constant endeavors. My husband has also taken up that cross in allowing me the privilege of living close to family while his job takes him an hour's drive away from home. Diligence and gallantry are not lacking in the men I know and love.[15]

In considering some of your own observations and life experiences, what examples of gallantry in men's relationships with women come to mind? Again, those may include, but are not limited to, interactions between parents, grandparents, uncles and aunts, neighbors, and friends.

_____

_____

_____

_____

_____

_____

---

[15] In all fairness to my younger brother, I must admit that, while his job has not taken him far from home, the constancy with which he has pursued his employment has set a great precedent for me in following my own occupational endeavors.

_____

_____

_____

How do you, as a man, apply gallantry in your life and in your interactions with the women you know?

_____

_____

_____

_____

_____

_____

_____

_____

In what ways do you perceive you might improve?

_____

_____

_____

_____

_____

How might those improvements enhance your life and your relationships?

_____

_____

_____

_____

_____

_____

_____

_____

Who might have thought that a simple word like chivalry could mean so much or that it could make such a difference in people's lives and relationships when put to good use? Honor, duty, valor, magnanimity and nobility, courtesy and kindness, helpfulness and service, as well as gallantry all hold fitting places in enhancing life and love relations. Taken as a whole, where in our world today does chivalry live on? It is most certainly in man's relationship with woman in day-to-day interactions and through small acts of kindness and service rendered. Therein, man becomes knight errant in the life of one whom he loves.

Laurels befitting a knight should, therefore, be his. Man must never be content merely to be the boyfriend or fiancée, the husband or father who mundanely accepts his roles and trudges somewhat disparagingly through the responsibilities associated with those. He must be the hero who was promised in all the tales of glory from days of yore. He must set his sights a little higher, reach a little further in attaining that goal, and the rewards will speak for themselves. He will be loved unquestioningly and know the place he's forever won in a woman's heart.

Chapter Two

To Win *His* Place beside *Her*

Thus far, we've discussed the benefits of reviving chivalry in man's quest for love and respect in the life of a woman. We've considered how he must perform the hero's part, how he must valiantly fight the battle and stand as knight errant with sword and buckler shining brightly in the sunlight, *but what of all his glory serves him well unless he is acknowledged for his accomplishments by the one whose heart he seeks to woo, the one to whom he bends the knee?* Woman harbors deep within the power to make or break the noble warrior, to lift him to exalted heights unknown or to send him crashing into depths of misery. The risk man takes in approaching her is that he may incur her disapproval rather than find the adoration for which he longs. Hence, many a valiant soldier may linger in the shadow of self-doubt before bravely mounting his trusted steed and sallying forth to meet his fear head on. Only by so doing does he win *his* place beside *her*.

In regard to overcoming his inhibitions as man sets forth to win a woman's heart, in what ways must he seek to approach her and to serve her? First, he must love her . . . *and love her in a way that she knows she is loved.* He must make himself vulnerable in his expressions of emotion and in showing forth his physical tenderness. Next, man must "let [his] light so shine" (Matthew 5:16)[16] that woman knows of his intellect, his ability to advise her and to teach her. To strengthen and enrich her life are goals to which he must attain. In addition, man's physical prowess, skill, and ability come into play in his pursuit of woman. His is considered to be the stronger sex. Why, then, should he not put his physical attributes to good use in benefiting the weaker? Finally, showing forth a willingness to stand on equal ground as friend, supporter, and companion is not without its merits. Being "equally yoked" (2 Corinthians 6:14)[17] to woman and serving her as she serves him is the pinnacle of man's union with the one he loves.

Love and Affection

Man must dare to love a woman. He must risk treating her with tenderness and speaking words of kindness and adoration. If a woman truly loves a man, she will bask in the warmth of his affection and offer her love in return. Many men may be in error in thinking that those gentle emotions are a weakness, in believing that a man must keep his more vulnerable feelings in check. Perhaps he perceives a measure of safety in doing so. However, by so doing, he masks part of what he can truly offer a woman, part of what is truly within. How can he gauge her willingness to yield to his approach if he is unwilling to fully reveal himself? Her response to his genuineness and openness will prove her worthy or unworthy of his continued pursuit.

---

[16] Corporation of the President of the Church of Jesus Christ of Latter-Day Saints. (1979). *The Holy Bible.* Salt Lake City, UT: The Church of Jesus Christ of Latter-Day Saints.
[17] *The Holy Bible.*

My own husband incurred some pain in a prior relationship that left him unwilling to share his tender emotions for a time. However, loneliness is a terrible price to pay to avoid the risk of sharing too much, and my husband has been fairly easily convinced, at least to a certain point, to reveal more of his true feelings and to grow closer to me emotionally. He still has a difficult time expressing his love in so many words, but all that he says and does reveals his love for me, and I am content with that. He expresses appreciation for the person that I am and the things that I do and maintains a constant adherence to a code of loyalty, and devotion, and honor. I know his love for me is true and that ours is a healing relationship for both of us.

Physical affection is also an important element in a relationship. Sexual hunger is a driving force that propels the sexes toward one another. Therein, a man may fear rejection in the physical advances he makes toward a woman. Affection is again the key. Gentle touches, and kisses, and words of praise and love can have somewhat of a sedating effect on a woman and may allow a full sexual experience to be more comforting and less physically distressing to her. Her physical anatomy in comparison with his may make the act of love seem like somewhat of an intrusion to her, and his awareness of her sensitivities and vulnerabilities may engender a heightened degree of gentleness on his part as he approaches her both physically and emotionally. Such an approach should lessen the likelihood of rejection and enhance his feelings of self-esteem as he succeeds in pleasing her as well as himself.

In considering some of your own observations and life experiences, what examples come to mind of men's love

*and affection in their relationships with women? Again,
those may include, but are not limited to, interactions
between parents, grandparents, uncles and aunts,
neighbors, and friends.*

_____

_____

_____

_____

_____

_____

_____

_____

_____

*How do you, as a man, apply love and affection in your life
and in your interactions with the women you know? (If the
relationship is sexual, perhaps I should say the "woman"
you know.)*

_____

_____

_____

_____

_____

_____

_____

_____

_____

In what ways do you perceive you might improve?

_____

_____

_____

_____

_____

_____

_____

How might those improvements enhance your life and your relationships?

_____

_____

_____

_____

_____

_____

_____

To Teach and to Advise

Some men may be replete with self-assurance and confidence in their level of education or training or in their overall degree of intelligence. Whereas, others may feel somewhat lacking in those respects. Regardless of the amount of information a man may possess or the areas in which he has invested himself in learning, there will always be things he can teach a woman that will help him to feel he is enhancing and enriching her life somehow. The ability to give of himself in instructing his partner and in sharing his interests is one means of loving her, and he would desire that she not reject him in his kind efforts.

My own husband has shown me things that have enhanced and enriched my life. He is an avid explorer of the great outdoors. He loves to hunt and to fish, to hike and to camp, and just to while away the hours in enjoying nature. Though my own father shared in all of those interests, I never allowed myself to be drawn into a love of the wilds until my husband came along and swept me off my feet and into the woods. Our very first outing was spent on the West Desert in north-western Utah and south-western Idaho. Whoever might have imagined that the desert could be so beautiful? The uneven terrain, the rivers of rock, stands of quaking aspen, sagebrush galore, and muted colors and fragrances filled my soul. I haven't been the same since being exposed to the sights and sounds, the tastes and smells of the desert. My mind and senses have been touched with a vision and a newfound feeling of wonderment that reminds me of childhood. That's what my husband gave to me. That's what he taught me just by sharing the things that he loves. I'm glad that he dared to reveal those things to me and that I accepted of him what he had to offer.

My husband has taught me other things, too, *things about cooking and eating in a healthier way and how to dress more in style with the latest fashions.* It's interesting that a man would know more about meal preparation and have a better fashion sense than a woman, but he's helped me to improve in those ways, and I appreciate him for it. I don't resent him. We each come endowed with our own interests and abilities, and it's through sharing those talents that we most come to appreciate ourselves and each other. A man can greatly enhance the life of a woman if he will only "put his best foot forward" in an effort to try.

A man can advise a woman, too. Though he may not always be the most self-assured in his ability to direct her as she sets out to make pertinent life decisions, his opinion is highly valued, and his objective viewpoint is extremely meaningful. Not only is he a separate person with ideas, values, and beliefs of his own, but his gender differences may shed an entirely different light on his ability to perceive things. Having that additional vantage point allows for added considerations to be taken before decisions are made or actions are engaged in. In daring to express his opinion, he shows a heightened regard for his companion and a deeper concern for her wellbeing. In pushing past fears of rejection, he can offer something of great meaning to her.

It wasn't my idea to write this book in the first place. It was my husband's. I believe it was an answer to his prayerful inquiry about how to resolve some of our mutual life concerns, *primarily financial*, as well as my own individual need for increased satisfaction in my work endeavors. Not only did he provide an outline for what the book should entail, *developing honor in and maintaining adherence to relationships*, but he advises me periodically as to what more I can add to enhance the finer details of my essay. *By the way, all my praise of him is entirely mine. He hasn't counseled me on any of that, though I don't think he minds how highly I think of him or how much I want to share my feelings with others.* I look to him for advice because I know how much he cares for me and how hard he tries to offer something of meaning and value through the ideas he shares. I'm glad he doesn't hold back on those. That would diminish his ability to be of assistance to me, and I would encourage any man to follow in his footsteps. I used to look to my father for advice, but he died shortly after I was married, and I'm glad to have another objective person to turn to in my life who can play that most important role for me.

In considering some of your own observations and life experiences, what examples come to mind of men's teaching and advising in their relationships with women? Again, those may include, but are not limited to, interactions between parents, grandparents, uncles and aunts, neighbors, and friends.

_____

_____

_____

_____

_____

_____

_____

_____

_____

How do you, as a man, apply teaching and advising in your life and in your interactions with the women you know?

_____

_____

_____

_____

_____

_____

_____

_____

In what ways do you perceive you might improve?

_____

_____

_____

How might those improvements enhance your life and your relationships?

"Let's Get Physical."[18]

    I used to pray for *a mechanic of my very own.* That's because I would get so frustrated with my own inability to maintain upkeep on my car or to fix things around my household that were routinely breaking. I'd put forth my best effort to try to correct a problem or pay someone else to do it, but it wasn't until my husband came along with all his splendid mechanical ability that I was able to put my mind to rest and know that all would be well from day to day and from place to place in the *humdrum world of fix-its.* I only say humdrum because fixing things has never been one of my greatest interests, though I find it entirely fascinating that someone else can do it . . . *and with such great expertise.* I was amazed as I witnessed on our very first date my husband's aptitude to repair things. As I mentioned before, we were in the West Desert and driving on some pretty uneven terrain when we got a flat tire. We would have been in somewhat of a fix, *no pun intended,* if my husband hadn't backed the vehicle partway up the hill and onto more level ground prior to jumping out and replacing that tire quicker than I could blink an eye. I'd never seen it done so well. *My prayers were answered . . .* thanks to my husband's willingness to learn how to do what I could not and to employ what he had learned in benefiting me. He continues to do so to this day.

    Any man can be a blessing in the life of a woman if he is willing to apply himself in developing his physical strengths and abilities. In so doing, he becomes more adept at offering her something of value that is unique from what

---

[18] Kipner, S., & Shaddick, T. (1981). Physical [Recorded by O. Newton-John]. On *Physical* [Cassett Tape, LP]. Universal City, CA: MCA.

she has traditionally been encouraged to learn and to do. If it is her desire to gain such knowledge and ability for herself, he can be a great asset in instructing and helping her along the way. In any regard, a man should not withhold his willingness to be of assistance to a woman in sharing his physical attributes with her. It is one way in which he can show his love and concern, and a woman who is worthy of his offering will also be accepting of it.

In considering some of your own observations and life experiences, what examples come to mind of men's sharing their physical attributes in their relationships with women? Again, those may include, but are not limited to, interactions between parents, grandparents, uncles and aunts, neighbors, and friends.

_____

_____

_____

_____

_____

_____

_____

_____

How do you, as a man, share your physical attributes in your life and in your interactions with the women you know?

_____

_____

_____

_____

_____

_____

_____

_____

_____

In what ways do you perceive you might improve?

_____

_____

_____

_____

_____

_____

_____

_____

How might those improvements enhance your life and your relationships?

_____

_____

_____

_____

_____

_____

_____

_____

_____

_____

The Friend She's Longed For

> *Of all the dreams of womankind,*
> *The dashing and the bold,*
> *There is but one that comes to mind,*
> *A friend to have and hold . . .*

There is no greater attainment in the life of a woman than to have the friendship and support of her male companion. Beyond the physical pleasure that is promised in the union between a man and a woman is a sense of being one in purpose, one in mind, of uplifting and upholding one another in sharing life's joys, facing its disappointments, and rising to meet its challenges. Without man, woman would be left alone and have no one with whom to share all that life brings her way. It is, therefore, necessary that he should prepare himself to be the friend, the loyal supporter, the companion *for whom she has longed*. Though it may seem an impossible task when considering the individual and gender differences inherent in such a partnership, it is feasible to achieve a state of oneness, and man must not be afraid of the merger.

At the beginning of our relationship, my husband used to tell me that the last thing in the world he wanted to be was *"my friend."* I think those words connoted somewhat of a diminished value and meaning for him in comparison with *"the love of my life."* However, whereas the tide of passion may ebb and flow in a relationship, the steady current of friendship, companionship, and support moves in a constant course. It is only natural for more intense feelings of love to be intermingled with more nurturing ones and for one's heated pursuit of a partner to be replaced with a more relaxed spirit of fun and play. After having been engaged in our relationship for over a decade now, my husband has gained a new sense of what friendship can really mean between a man and a woman, of what it feels like to have a companion close by in times of loss or sickness or to have her tagging along on all his life's excursions and adventures. Husband and wife, parent and child, and brother and sister roles become intertwined. I believe that kind of versatility is what my husband and I value the most about our relationship, and we look forward to the coming years together with hopeful anticipation of all that we can offer to and receive from one another.

I know of a man, a friend of my father, who was a recent widower at the time I met him. He told me the story of his life, of the hardships he encountered in being raised by a relative who did not truly love him, and of finding himself having to look after his own needs from a very young age. He recounted that the woman he eventually married grew up in a similar set of unfortunate circumstances and that they were for one another more than just husband and wife. She was "mother" to him, and he was "father" to her. He lost far more than his wife when she died. He lost the one who loved him, who supported him, and who nurtured him throughout his adult years, both in his youth and in his old age. His sadness at losing her seemed to span the universe, and, yet, his satisfaction at knowing how deeply and how well he had been loved appeared to sustain him and to carry him forward in meeting the challenges that lay ahead in his widowhood. That kind of love never dies.

Therefore, in regard to the friendship, the companionship, and support a man can offer a woman, their worth is far more than can be surmised in a glance. It may take years of careful study, evaluation, and personal experience to realize their value as the highest attainment he can achieve in *his* relationship with *her*.

In considering some of your own observations and life experiences, what examples come to mind of men's friendship, companionship, and support in their relationships with women? Again, those may include, but are not limited to, interactions between parents, grandparents, uncles and aunts, neighbors, and friends.

_____

_____

_____

_____

_____

_____

_____

_____

_____

How do you, as a man, apply friendship, companionship, and support in your life and in your interactions with the women you know?

_____

_____

_____

_____

_____

_____

_____

In what ways do you perceive you might improve?

_____

_____

_____

_____

_____

_____

_____

_____

How might those improvements enhance your life and your relationships?

_____

_____

_____

_____

_____

_____

_____

_____

_____

So, in regard to man's desire to gain a woman's acceptance, he must be unto her "a man for all seasons."[19] He must be the one to whom she turns for love and affection, the one who enhances and enriches her life through extending his teaching and advice, the one who lends a hand to mend all that's broken, and the friend, companion, and giver of support for whom she's longed and deemed necessary to walk beside her in this life's

[19] Zinnemann, F. (Producer/Director). (1966). *A Man for All Seasons* [Motion Picture]. United Kingdom: Highland Films.

journey. It is within man's grasp to give so much in his relationship with woman and within hers to accept of his offering.

Chapter 3

To Hear and Understand Her
And Speak to Her in Turn

———————

Being able to communicate effectively with his partner is a must as a man develops a meaningful relationship with a woman. He needs to be able to hear and understand what she has to say and to convey that understanding back to her in a way that she knows he is listening. He must also be able to say what is on his mind and in his heart so that she can hear and understand him without being hurt or offended in the process. Communication is an intricate interchange between a man and a woman and is an important enough part of their interaction that it must be handled with all delicacy if *he* hopes to win *her* heart. Included in this chapter are some time-tested rules of communication that may tip the balance in a man's favor as he approaches the woman of his dreams and attempts to woe her with his *glorious gift of gab*.

To Hear and Understand

To be heard and understood is each woman's goal in self-expression. *She* feels a satisfaction unlike any other at times when *he* is willing to stand beside her and listen to her joys and sorrows, her losses and triumphs, her pleasures and pains. It doesn't fully matter what comes knocking at her life's door as long as he is there to comfort and uphold her, to exult in her victories, and to soothe her strains. She perceives that all is well as long as her source of strength and support is with her, *but how is it that she knows he is listening, that he truly hears and understands what she has to say?*

There are a few simple *but not always well-known* rules of communication that may very well aid a man in his quest to be the kind of listener a woman will adore. According to Robert Carkhuff,[20] a relationship expert who did most of his work in decades past, *active listening* entails not only hearing *but expressing back a reflection of* the content, feeling, and meaning of what has been spoken. Reflection is proof that a man has heard a woman and is trying to understand what she has said. The depth of attention required in reflection reveals an uncommon interest on *his* part that may very well ignite an equal interest in *her*.

What does it mean to *reflect content?* Content is merely what has been stated and is likely the most easily understood part of a woman's expression. If she tells a man she's had a hard day on the job, he may say, *"I'm sorry to hear your day has been so difficult for you."* Not only has he captured the essence of what she has told him, but he has conveyed some concern for her as well by saying, *"I'm sorry."* His compassion will intrigue her and draw her closer to him. Again, reflection of content is a restatement of what has been spoken.

Reflection of feeling, on the other hand, may require a bit more discernment on *his* part. It demands an ability to

---

[20] Truax, C. B., & Carkhuff, R. R. (1967). *Toward Effective Counseling and Psychotherapy: Training and Practice.* Chicago, IL: Aldine Publishing Company.

infer what *she* is feeling based on what she is saying and then to express those feelings in his own words. So, if a woman says she's had a hard day on the job, a man may reply, *"I'm sorry to hear your day has been so difficult for you. You seem to be feeling pretty down about things."* Therein, he expresses an even deeper level of understanding than what is based solely on the content of her expression. A man displays additional concern for a woman by sharing his insights into how she might be feeling. That may further endear *him* to *her*.

In regard to reflection of feeling, it is possible to be in error when inferring another's emotions or in choosing just the right words to describe those. A man should be prepared to be informed by a woman if his words don't fully capture the essence of her affect. He doesn't have to be right every time. It's the effort he puts into trying to empathize with her that counts. That's the way to win her heart.

Finally, *reflection of meaning* requires more than a man's ability to restate what a woman has spoken or to express his insights into her emotions. It involves developing an understanding as to why she might be feeling the way she does. For instance, a woman tells a man she's had a hard day on the job. He reflects the content of what she has said by saying, *"I'm sorry to hear your day has been so difficult for you."* In reflecting her feelings, he states, *"You seem to be feeling pretty down about things."* He takes his analysis a step further in reflecting meaning. He may have known she was expecting to get a raise or a job promotion that day. He may ask her, *"Did you hear back from your boss about the raise (or job promotion)?"* She may say, *"Yes. I didn't get it.*" He may then complete his reflection by saying, *"I can see why you're feeling so down. You really wanted that raise (or job promotion)."* She can either agree or disagree with that assumption, but the process has begun. He is earnestly seeking to understand how she feels and why she feels that way. His interest can only serve to reveal a concern that will draw her in rather than push her away.

All that has been discussed about listening, thus far, can be summed up in three simple statements:

1) *So, what you're saying is . . .*
2) *And the way you feel about that is . . .*
3) *And you feel that way because . . .*

It's hard to go wrong when using a time-tested formula such as the one developed by Carkhuff. However, there are a few missteps which can be made in the process of active listening if proper care isn't taken. Sometimes, people hear only what they want to hear. They often come equipped with misconceived notions. Let's say, for instance, that a woman is telling a man *she needs to spend money on some necessary household items.* What he hears her saying is that *she wants to waste money on things she doesn't need.* In that scenario, there is obviously a difference of opinions, which may be colored by some value judgments on both parts.

It is important not to let one's own judgments stand in the way of truly listening to what another has to say. So, take a deep breath, and simply reflect the content, feeling, and meaning expressed by your partner. You want to win her heart, don't you? Then give her center stage. Let her talk. You just listen and reflect. You might say something like, *"I know you'd really like to get those new appliances for the kitchen. I can see it's a frustration for you to have to do without them. Work around the house would be a lot easier with a few more of the conveniences."* How hard was that, and what did it cost you more than a few moments of your time and a listening ear? It's not necessarily a matter of giving in to her demands. Rather, you simply need to stand in her shoes for a few moments before presenting your case so that she knows you care about her thoughts and feelings, her wants and needs. Now that she feels listened to and understood, it's your turn to talk and hers to listen. Hopefully, she'll follow your lead. It's not just working the bugs out of a relationship that makes it strong. It's how you go about doing so.

Another common mistake made in listening to other people is that, oftentimes, feelings get dropped entirely out of the equation. We, as human beings, are not necessarily accustomed to dealing with feelings. It seems that we rarely take time out to ponder our own emotions let alone consider someone else's affect, and by no means do we rack our brains trying to come up with just the right words to describe those inward states of being. However, like it or not, we all have feelings, and I think that most of us would be in agreement that we wouldn't mind having those acknowledged once in a while. Therefore, though Carkhuff's assignment may not be such an easy one after all, it might very well be worth investing a little time and effort into learning more about emotions and how to talk about those.

An additional error a man may make in embarking upon Carkhuff's listening process is that *he* might infer all the wrong reasons why *she* feels as she does. He may be basing his perceptions on his own experience rather than trying to gain an understanding of where she is coming from. In that case, asking questions can be a powerful tool in gaining a proper perspective into her world. Can a man go wrong by asking a woman, *"What is it that's making you feel so sad?"* I don't think so. Can she help but appreciate him for his thoughtfulness and concern? Again, I think the chances are pretty slim. So, when in doubt, check it out . . . *with some pertinent questions.*

Carkhuff was a wise man, and his formulas have been put to the test in different professions designed to help others throughout the world and across generations of time. They seem to be tried and true. *Now, let them help you.*

In considering some of your own observations and life experiences, what examples come to mind of men's active listening in their relationships with women? Again, those may include, but are not limited to, interactions between parents, grandparents, uncles and aunts, neighbors, and friends.

_____

_____

_____

_____

_____

_____

_____

_____

_____

How do you, as a man, apply active listening in your life and in your interactions with the women you know?

_____

_____

_____

_____

_____

_____

_____

In what ways do you perceive you might improve?

_____

_____

_____

_____

_____

_____

_____

How might those improvements enhance your life and your relationships?

_____

_____

_____

_____

_____

_____

_____

_____

To Speak to Her

Thus far, we've considered some of the finer points of *receptive communication*, or how a man might actively listen to his partner by reflecting the content, feeling, and meaning inherent in her verbal expressions, as a means of growing closer in their relationship with one another. Of equal importance is *expressive communication*, or man's ability to *express* himself *positively and assertively*[21] through the things he says. By exercising assertive-

---

[21] Palmer, P., & Shondeck, B. L. (1977). *Liking Myself.* San Luis Obispo, CA: Impact Publishers.

communication skills, his thoughts and feelings, his wants and needs are brought into his partner's awareness without imposing upon her a sense of being responsible or to blame for those.   In other words, he does not put her on the defensive in his manner of communicating. He allows her the opportunity to hear and understand him without necessarily becoming hurt or angry in the process, especially when broaching upon sensitive subject matter.

For instance, a man may be angry about a household expenditure that he feels was unnecessary and that he was not consulted about beforehand.   In that case, it is imperative for him to express from his viewpoint the content, feeling, and meaning related to the expenditure. He may say, *"I came home from work and found a new washer and dryer in the laundry room. They were a lot more expensive than what I would have purchased myself."* That's the content related to the expenditure. He may then say, *"I'm really angry."*   That's the related feeling. Finally, he might add, *"I wasn't consulted about any of that, and I want to be included in making those kinds of decisions."* That's the related meaning, or reason, for his distress. He assertively expressed the content, feeling, and meaning inherent in his perspective of the situation through the use of *"I" statements.*   Therein, he maintained ownership of his thoughts and feelings, his wants and needs. He may then have offered an invitation for his partner to do likewise, and the two could have worked toward a solution to whatever discrepancies may have emerged in their expressed viewpoints.   That type of expression opens up a door to communication and potential problem solving that may very well have remained shut if the woman had been put on the defensive.

For example, the man's expression could just as easily have gone as follows: *"You bought a new washer and dryer without my approval. You spent way more money than I ever would have condoned. You'd better make sure those items are returned to the store by the time I get home from work tomorrow."* There are a number of problems inherent in that type of communication. First, the man neglected to be assertive and to take responsibility for his thoughts, his feelings, and the reasons he felt the way he did by failing to make use of *"I"* statements. In addition, he focused more on what the woman had done by placing blame and responsibility on her with *"you"* statements. Finally, he attempted to impose a solution on her rather than opening up a line of communication by giving her a chance to speak to him and by possibly engaging in some problem solving.[22]

Assertive communication of content, feeling, and meaning can be outlined in the same three steps as active listening:

1) *When . . . happens,*
2) *I feel . . .*
3) *Because . . .*

Though the process of positively and assertively expressing oneself may seem fairly straightforward at first glance, as in the case with active listening, a man may encounter some problems in his quest to relay his thoughts and feelings, his wants and needs to a woman. First, she may not choose to see things from his perspective or avail herself of the opportunity to stand in his shoes. He may

---

[22] Problem solving will be discussed at length in Chapter Six.

encounter a roadblock in his attempts to be listened to and understood by her because of a lack of ability or experience on her part in active listening or due to her firmly held beliefs which stand in opposition to his own. Second, he may find it difficult to express himself emotionally, and some time and effort may be required in learning how to verbalize his feelings and, potentially, in overcoming inhibitions about discussing those. Third, a man may not always understand why he feels the way he does let alone expect someone else to, and some soul searching may be necessary as he attempts to gain further insight and awareness into his own psyche. However, anticipating that the potential benefits of being open and honest in *his* communication with *her* may be great as they strive toward achieving a mutual understanding, he may certainly want to put forth his best effort to try.

In considering some of your own observations and life experiences, what examples come to mind of men's positive and assertive expression in their relationships with women? Again, those may include, but are not limited to, interactions between parents, grandparents, uncles and aunts, neighbors, and friends.

_____

_____

_____

_____

_____

_____

_____

_____

How do you, as a man, apply positive and assertive expression in your life and in your interactions with the women you know?

_____

_____

_____

_____

_____

_____

_____

_____

In what ways do you perceive you might improve?

_____

_____

_____

_____

_____

_____

_____

_____

How might those improvements enhance your life and your relationships?

_____

_____

_____

_____

_____

_____

_____

_____

Both active listening and positive and assertive self-expression are skills required in the process of communication as a man approaches a woman. The more skilled he becomes, the more receptive of his attempts she should grow to be. In time, a comfortable and expected interchange should develop between them that will enhance their relationship meaningfully.

In sum, Part One of this book has emphasized three fundamental needs which a man seeks to fulfill as he embarks upon his quest for companionship with the woman of his dreams. First, he looks to win her love and respect by conducting himself most chivalrously. Second, he strives for acceptance as he seeks to meet the many roles associated with his gender. Third, he attempts to achieve a mutual degree of understanding by establishing with his partner a line of communication that will facilitate not only an interchange of information through positive and assertive self-expression but also a sense of being truly heard by one another through the use of active-listening skills. By so doing, our brave knight enhances the likelihood that victory will be won in *his* pursuit of everlasting happiness with *her*.

Part Two

. . . And to Hold"

Chapter Four

Wherein Does Man Glory?

Part One of this book focused on Roger's three fundamental principles of relationship in man's pursuit of woman: 1) attaining her love and respect, 2) winning her acceptance, and 3) developing a mutual understanding. Part Two covers an equally challenging aspect of man's interaction with woman and one that he may fail despite having attained all his heart's desire. It is his ability to retain what he has rightfully won through his diligent efforts by embracing personal attributes that will contribute to the longevity of *his* partnership with *her*, by establishing a mutually acceptable degree of interconnectedness, and by learning to assist in resolving life's problems as they arise.

The present chapter will reveal those qualities thought to enhance longevity and contribute to permanence in man's union. It is essential for him to acquire a spirit of contentment and satisfaction with what he has attained, to engender a sense of appreciation and gratitude for his current situation, and to adhere to a code of loyalty and devotion to the one he loves. As noted in the forward to the book, what good is it for man *to climb to the top of the tallest snowy mountain if all he can do is long for scorching deserts once he has arrived?* So, too, in forming human ties, there must be a sense of stability in the connection at hand. After all, *wherein does man glory if it is not in the prize?*

Peace and Contentment

According to Webster, to be content is to have "the desires limited by what one has." Webster refers to *contentment* as being a *passive state* in which there is an "absence of fretting or craving" and "a resting or satisfaction of mind without disquiet or craving for something else; acquiescence in one's own circumstances." Contentment is oftentimes equated with *peace*, which, according to Webster, is "a state of quiet or tranquility; calm, quietness, or repose; freedom from war or hostility; a cessation of hostilities; absence of strife; tranquility of mind; harmony; serenity; public tranquility and order." It seems only natural in relationships that a sense of peace and contentment should emerge through an *absence of hostility*. Therein is one ingredient essential to man's peaceable existence with woman.

Of all the peaceful unions which I have observed in my lifetime, one emerges as being unique in its degree of perfection. It was the marriage relationship between my maternal grandparents, both born near the turn of the Twentieth Century, joined to one another in their twenties, and having lived together for decades prior to my birth. I don't remember ever having heard them argue or speak an unkind word to each other. All I recall are the terms of praise and endearment which they offered one another. Grandpa had a special nickname for my grandmother. He called her "Vernie," which was short for her middle name, LaVern. No one else called her "Vernie." That was just Grandpa's special familiarity for her, and it meant enough to Grandma that she mentioned it to me on one occasion. That was something unique between the two of them.

Another tale she told me was how my grandfather used to make the long trek between where they were then living in Logan, Utah, and my grandmother's place of origin in Ogden, Utah, to visit her family soon after their marriage when she was feeling down and missing them. What would be an hour's journey in a modern automobile on today's roadways was likely far more time consuming then. Neither automobiles nor roadways were as user friendly in those days as they are now. One might even think of them as having been somewhat treacherous and uncomfortable, especially on one particular occasion when my grandmother was in labor with my mother, her second child, and journeying home to be near family and to have the assistance of the doctor who had delivered her firstborn, a son, while giving birth once again. Even in our day, the thin and winding stretch of roadway they traveled then through Sardine Canyon is considered to be one of the most deadly in our nation. In her reminiscing, Grandma used to tell me that not just any man would have done the things for her that my grandfather did. Special endearments and continued appreciation for deeds long past were means of breeding a spirit of peace and contentment in their household.

In considering some of your own observations and life experiences, what examples of peace and contentment in men's relationships with women come to mind? Again, those may include, but are not limited to, interactions between parents, grandparents, uncles and aunts, neighbors, and friends.

_____

_____

_____

_____

_____

_____

_____

How do you, as a man, apply peace and contentment in your life and in your interactions with the women you know?

_____

_____

_____

_____

_____

_____

_____

_____

In what ways do you perceive you might improve?

_____

_____

_____

_____

_____

_____

_____

_____

How might those improvements enhance your life and your relationships?

_____

_____

_____

_____

_____

_____

_____

_____

Satisfaction – What's the "Language" of Your Love?[23]

Whereas contentment is considered by Webster to be a passive state, *satisfaction* is thought to be *active* in that it is "an active feeling of pleasure" gained through the "fulfillment of desires, demands, or needs." It is the "gratification or pleasure occasioned by some fact or circumstance; the cause of such gratification." It is true that one individual may gain a sense of satisfaction from means entirely different from another. In regard to love relationships, satisfaction is thought to stem from a variety of sources, or ways of giving and receiving love. There are those who relish *physical pleasure* and gain satisfaction therein. Others cherish *words of love and appreciation*. Still, others look to *helpful gestures or deeds* to ensure their love is real. *Gifts and tokens* are, yet, another means of bringing love to life. In addition, sharing *meaningful moments* has its intrinsic value in romantic attachments. It is vital to know both your own "love language" as well as that of your lady as you journey to find love and satisfaction in your relationship together.

In considering "love languages," a story comes to mind about a husband and wife who were so embittered in their relationship that they could not even speak a civil word to one another, and, so, they were counseled to remain in silence. It's hard to say just how long their speechless vigil lasted, as I don't recall every detail of the story. However, the couple must have been silent for quite some time before a most curious thing happened. One day, the husband, a farmer by profession, uprooted some weeds that were of

---

[23] Chapman, G. D. (1992). *The Five Love Languages: How to Express Heartfelt Commitment to Your Mate.* Chicago, IL: Northfield Publishing.

special interest to him, put them in a glass jar, and placed them in his kitchen. His wife, unaware of his intent in bringing the weeds into her home, affixed added meaning to his action that brought their ongoing feud to an abrupt halt. She thought they were a token of his love for her and acted accordingly. That evening, not only was a bounteous meal awaiting the farmer at day's end, but his wife, beaming with happiness over her husband's newfound interest in her, was also prepared to greet him in her finest apparel and with her hair neatly styled. She spoke words of kindness and appreciation for his gift. He was in awe at the splendid impact his simple gesture had on his wife and her feelings for him and insured that, from then on, tokens of his love were often forthcoming, as he knew what they meant to both of them. He had unintentionally stumbled upon his wife's "love language," and she had also discovered his.

In considering some of your own observations and life experiences, what examples come to mind of men's developing satisfaction and discovering both similarities and differences in "love languages" in their relationships with women? Again, those may include, but are not limited to, interactions between parents, grandparents, uncles and aunts, neighbors, and friends.

_____

_____

_____

_____

_____

_____

_____

_____

_____

How do you, as a man, apply satisfaction and "love languages" in your life and in your interactions with the women you know?

_____

_____

_____

_____

_____

_____

_____

_____

In what ways do you perceive you might improve?

_____

_____

_____

_____

_____

_____

_____

_____

_____

How might those improvements enhance your life and your relationships?

_____

_____

_____

_____

_____

_____

_____

_____

"Johnny Lingo's Eight-Cow Wife"

It seems that both contentment and satisfaction are enhanced by a sense of appreciation or gratitude for what one has. To *appreciate* is "to be grateful for; to regard highly; to esteem or value properly; to set a just price, value, or estimate on." It also means "to rise in value; to become of more value." Appreciation is seen as being synonymous with *gratitude*, which is thought to be "a warm and friendly appreciation of a kindness or a favor received; thankfulness; gratefulness." Those definitions remind me of the story of Johnny Lingo.[24]   As the tale is told, Johnny, both a wise and a fair trader in the islands of the Pacific, paid far more to obtain the right to marry his childhood sweetheart, Sarita, *also known as Mahana in the movie version of the story*,[25] than the islanders ever thought she was worth.   "Plain," "skinny," "afraid of her own shadow" were terms they used to describe her, and, yet, no greater price was ever offered for a woman on the islands than was given for her. The effects were truly remarkable. Sarita became unto Johnny all he imaged her to be, "beautiful," "glorious," and filled with "a pride to which no one could deny her the right," as she was so highly valued by her husband. Because Johnny loved Sarita and treated her as though she were worth more than any other, she rose to meet her greatest potential and became unto him all he ever dreamed of.   Appreciation and gratitude both were major players in that account.   Johnny appreciated Sarita for all that she was and ever could be, and she showed her gratitude unto him by accepting his esteem.

It is amazing to feel the effects of being truly valued by another. I am fortunate to partake of that blessing in my own life due to the constant love and affection which my husband offers me.   A day never goes by without my hearing something wonderful from him about me. He tells me that I'm "beautiful," that I'm "capable," and that I'm a "kind" and "good" person, wife, and mother. Those words mean more to me than anything. They give me the strength to face daily challenges and go on with my life even when things seem harsh and unfriendly because I know who I am

---

[24] McGerr, P. (1965). *Johnny Lingo & the Eight-Cow Wife*. Newport Beach, CA: Kenning House.
[25] Whitaker, W. O. (Producer/Director). (1969). *Johnny Lingo* [Motion Picture]. United States: Brigham Young University.

in the eyes of my husband and I am confident that will never change. It doesn't matter what anyone else thinks of me. As long as I have my husband beside me, I am somewhat invincible. A man can do that for the woman he loves. He can give her the confidence it takes to face the good and the bad in her life and to conquer it all.

In considering some of your own observations and life experiences, what examples of appreciation and gratitude in men's relationships with women come to mind? Again, those may include, but are not limited to, interactions between parents, grandparents, uncles and aunts, neighbors, and friends.

_____

_____

_____

_____

_____

_____

_____

_____

_____

How do you, as a man, apply appreciation and gratitude in your life and in your interactions with the women you know?

_____

_____

_____

_____

_____

_____

_____

_____

_____

In what ways do you perceive you might improve?

_____

_____

_____

_____

_____

_____

_____

_____

_____

How might those improvements enhance your life and your relationships?

_____

_____

_____

_____

_____

_____

_____

_____

_____

After the Flower Has Gone

In regard to retaining what one has in a relationship, it may be of benefit to consider interactions between men and women that span the entirety of their adult lives. What are some ingredients in addition to contentment and satisfaction, appreciation and gratitude that contribute to such longevity? Loyalty and devotion are characteristics that come to mind in answer to that question. In quoting Webster, to be *loyal* is to be "faithful to one's oath, engagements, or obligations; faithful to one's allegiance, as to a sovereign, government, or state; faithful to any person or thing conceived as imposing obligations." Taking the analysis a step further, to be *faithful* is to be "strict in the performance of duty; unswervingly devoted; loyal to one's promises; trustworthy." *Devotion* is equated with "dedication; consecration," and an "earnest attachment to a cause or person."

I have known of individuals who have remained loyal, faithful, and devoted in their love relations even years after their loved ones have passed on. They have lived with the memories of their dearly departed and have cherished their time spent together in years gone by. One man, in particular, comes to mind. His dedication to his wife seemed undying as the two of them tenderly cared for her granddaughter, a young girl handicapped in her infancy by the negligent treatment of an unworthy caregiver. Together, the couple ensured that all the child's needs were provided for, including the love and security that was offered in their home. When his wife fell ill, the man lovingly cared for both her and her grandchild until the time came that his wife could remain in mortality no longer. At that time, he also lost claim to the little girl, as she was of no blood relation to him. However, he has continued to live his life in memory of the ones he loves. He attempts to narrow the distance between him and them by maintaining adherence to the dictates of his own conscience, by staying true to his religious ideals, by being kind and courteous in his treatment of others, and by abiding alone with the images of wife and child to sustain him.

By no means, however, is that man independent in his faithful vigil. There are many who endure some amount of loneliness and difficulty following the passing of loved ones and who continue to honor their memories through their daily walks of life. Some continue to abide singly. Others may form new ties through romantic attachments while reserving in their hearts a special place for those who have moved beyond their reach. What about those of us who currently live in love relations? Can we look to the examples set by those who have lost the objects of their affection and, yet, somehow continue to love unendingly? It is that kind of love and faithful devotion to which we must strive if our current connections are to remain strong and impenetrable through time, which is the true test of any relationship.

In considering some of your own observations and life experiences, what examples of loyalty, faithfulness, and devotion in men's relationships with women come to mind? Again, those may include, but are not limited to, interactions between parents, grandparents, uncles and aunts, neighbors, and friends.

_____

_____

_____

_____

_____

_____

_____

_____

_____

How do you, as a man, apply loyalty, faithfulness, and devotion in your life and in your interactions with the women you know?

_____

_____

_____

_____

_____

_____

_____

_____

_____

In what ways do you perceive you might improve?

_____

_____

_____

_____

_____

_____

_____

How might those improvements enhance your life and your relationships?

_____

_____

_____

_____

_____

_____

_____

_____

_____

In touching upon the elements considered to be essential in enhancing longevity and establishing permanence in a relationship, the present chapter has focused upon personal attributes of contentment and satisfaction, appreciation and gratitude, loyalty and devotion. To find peace and enjoyment within one's union, to value and extol it for being the miraculous blessing that it is, and to remain true to one's feelings and commitments over time are the ingredients that lasting bonds are made of.

Chapter Five

To Be as One

Establishing a reciprocally convenient degree of interconnectedness in a relationship is a job from which no couple can escape . . . *but one that is necessary in ensuring their union will endure.* Though some pairings may find it to be an easier task than others do, there is always some work involved in coming to terms with just how enmeshed *he* hopes to be with *her* and *she* with *him* as they traverse life's paths together. That is one of their many challenges to be faced. In addition, the degree of support they will offer one another is, as yet, undetermined at the outset of their companionship and a question that must be answered as they strive to attain longevity and permanence.

My Buddy

In holding fast to the love relationship which he has rightfully won, man must be mindful of the degree to which he seeks to interconnect his life with that of his lady, for many a fair heart may languish should their actions and desires on that account not be as one. I have heard it said by one very wise in the ways of manhood and womanhood both that to lack unison in that regard is to be assured of trouble in the coming years . . . *if not of certain doom.* That man was not my father, but father he was to me in sharing the knowledge that only years of observation and experience could impart. He told me the degree to which a man chooses to share his time, his personal space, and interests with the woman of his dreams must be in conformity with her own expectations if his dreams are to become reality. It is not to say that he must be captive to her every whim, but prisoner he will be if his desire is to "run the gauntlets"[26] of life alone as she sits pining and awaiting his welcomed return while, all along, she intends for him to be seated by her side and dutifully attending to her every need. It is not the degree to which he avails himself to her that will determine the level of harmony within their relationship but the extent to which they hold their views in common.

The gentleman to whom I referred in the preceding paragraph was both a religious and a secular advisor in the field of counseling. He had dealt with many situations in which men and women had approached him for instruction on how to improve their relationships with one another. The counsel that he offered was depicted by a series of paired circles which he drew to illustrate the degrees of interconnectedness couples can attain in their joint interactions. He first portrayed a relationship in which there was very little overlap. In essence, the circles barely touched. That might be a representation of a pairing in which the man and woman have relatively few interests in common and in which they are both seemingly content to live their separate lives but to come together as occasion requires in meeting their mutual needs. While such an illusive approach to oneness may not match the expectations of the majority of couples, it may be enough to content some and to provide the objective distance

[26] origin and meaning cited on www.phrases.org.uk/meanings

necessary in maintaining peace and harmony within those unions.

The second set of circles depicted a relationship in which there was almost complete overlap. There was very little space in either circle that was not immersed in the other. Some relationships are like that. The man and the woman spend almost all their time together in mutual pursuits at home, at work, and in their recreational endeavors. They share most, if not all, their interests in common, *or hopefully they do*. If not, either one or the other partner is likely to be quite miserable in his or her forced involvement in the other's enjoyments. Either way, wherever he is bound to be seen, so is she, and vice versa. There is a strong degree of enmeshment in such relationships, which may be necessary in providing the level of comfort and support that some individuals desire. That only becomes problematic when one or the other partner becomes limited in his or her personal achievements or when either desires more freedom and independence.

The third set of circles represented by far the majority of relationships. The degree of overlap fell midway between the first and second depictions and alluded to the greater amount of flexibility which most couples desire in their interrelatedness with one another. While most individuals seek to share a certain percentage of their time, personal space, and interests with their companion, *the object of their undying love and devotion*, they also find a great deal of contentment or necessity in following more singular paths. It may not always be feasible for a man and a woman to engage in all their endeavors together. Their differing backgrounds may engender separate likes and dislikes and dissimilar qualifications to take part in the same vocations or avocations. It may also be essential in meeting the needs of the relationship for each partner to play a distinct role that will add to their degree of separation. For example, one partner might be more homebound with the children while the other is more outbound with employment. In addition, most people are inclined to want to have some alone time to relax, to pursue their individual pleasures, and simply to enjoy being who they are as separate beings from the ones they love. Irrespective of the reason, most couples' degree of enmeshment is represented by the last depiction.

In regard to maintaining the necessary degree of contentment and satisfaction required to enhance longevity in a relationship, it is imperative that both *he* and *she* hold similar views on the amount of time, personal space, and interests the two of them hope to share in common. Otherwise, a never-ending row may ensue. I am afraid that was one area in my own parents' marriage that contributed to some contentions within our household as I was growing up. My father was a man who loved to find adventure kicking around in the sticks and gathering rocks. He was a geologist at heart and through his training . . . *if not in his primary profession*. Therefore, he pursued that field as a *principle avocation*. "Picking rocks" was his favorite pastime and one that often took him far from home and family for days at a time. My mother, on the other hand, learned to hate rocks as her *principle rival* for my father's time and attention. Whereas some women may have welcomed having time alone to tend to necessary household chores and childcare responsibilities, *if not to do their own thing*, my mother was embittered toward my father for his lack of support during his excursions. Other women may have jumped at the chance to tag along on such "rock-picking" adventures. My mother, on the other hand, was more of a homebody who didn't care to rough it in the great outdoors. Neither parent was wrong in his or her desires, my father for seeking greater independence due to my mother's relative lack of interest in his pursuits or my mother for wanting more of his time and attention to be devoted to her and their mutual responsibilities at home. The problem arose as a result of their conflicting perspectives on that point. It would seem that my father's quest for satisfaction through pursuing his interests diminished my mother's contentment in her home life and vice versa.

How might my parents' quandary have been prevented? One truth that my father shared with me is that "marriage is not a bed of roses," or, if it is, *be prepared to encounter some thorns.* I think what he was trying to tell me is that no couple's relationship is without its problems. He had certainly learned that in his own marriage and could likely perceive the validity of that statement in other unions as well. Be that as it may, I do believe there are ways to prevent the misfortune that my parents experienced due to their disparate views on togetherness. *When in doubt, check it out.* *He* and *she* both have every opportunity before their vows are spoken to explore one another's perspective on how enmeshed they hope to be in each other's life. *Take some time to figure that out before rushing into things.* Investing a little time and a bit of thought into that matter prior to "jumping the broom"[27] is a small price to pay to prevent a lifetime of misery or a broken family. That is perhaps the best advice that can be

---

[27] reference to an African-American wedding tradition

given on that subject. I'm sure you've heard what they say about "*an ounce of prevention.*" The only other solution is "*a pound of cure.*"[28] In that case, one or the other partner or both may have to sacrifice personal desires for the good of the relationship. It becomes quite a balancing act to ensure that neither spouse becomes overly burdened in that regard.

In considering some of your own observations and life experiences, what examples of enmeshment in men's relationships with women come to mind and to what degree? How do men's and women's similarities and differences in their viewpoints on togetherness either contribute to or diminish the degree of peace and harmony within those unions? Again, those may include, but are not limited to, interactions between parents, grandparents, uncles and aunts, neighbors, and friends.

_____

_____

_____

_____

_____

_____

_____

_____

[28] Reference *Random House Dictionary of Popular Proverbs and Sayings* by Gregory Y. Titelman (1996) for the origin and meaning of that phrase. – as cited on www.phrases.org.uk/meanings

To what extent do you, as a man, perceive that you are enmeshed in your interactions with the women you know? (Again, perhaps I should say the "woman" you know.) How do similarities and differences in your viewpoints on togetherness either contribute to or diminish the degree of peace and harmony within your union?

_____

_____

_____

_____

_____

_____

_____

_____

In what ways do you perceive you might improve?

_____

_____

_____

_____

_____

_____

How might those improvements enhance your life and your relationships?

_____

_____

_____

_____

_____

_____

_____

_____

"How Do I Live Without You?"[29] [30]

In conjunction with the concept of enmeshment is the notion of interdependence. Webster defines *dependence* as "a state of being dependent; connection and support; mutual connection; interrelation; a state of relying on another for support or existence; a state of being subject to

---

[29] Warren, D. (1997). How Do I Live [Recorded by L. Rimes]. On *You Light Up My Life: Inspirational Songs* [CD, Cassette Tape], Nashville, TN: Curb.

[30] Warren, D. (1997). How Do I Live [Recorded by T. Yearwood]. On *Songbook: A Collection of Hits* [CD, Cassette Tape], Nashville, TN: MCA.

the operation of any other cause; reliance; confidence; trust." The degree of interdependence in a relationship equates with the extent to which each partner's needs are being met by the other. Those requirements can be broadly defined, at least in part, as encompassing the temporal means necessary to sustain life. Shelter and warmth, food and water, clothing, household and personal-care items all must be provided for within the realm of one's partnership. Historically, men have taken on the role of furnishing those necessities, and women the function of ensuring they are put to their best use within the household in meeting the needs of all its members. In today's society, however, the greater likelihood is that men and women both take part in supplying necessary means to meet temporal needs as well as ensuring they are utilized properly. Thus, we see an interdependence of a different sort emerging with the evolution of our culture and the diminished distinction between traditional male and female roles.

Of equal importance to meeting the temporal needs of the partnership is the desire to be loved and supported within one's union. S*he* looks to *him*, as *he* to *her*, in seeking fulfillment of those yearnings. While love, affection, friendship, support, and companionship have been touched upon in an earlier chapter, they deserve to be mentioned once again here. In addition to fulfilling one's physical desires through sexual intimacy, the relationship between *him* and *her* is a place where emotions are pampered, intellects are stimulated, and spirits can soar. Interdependence connotes a healthy sort of leaning upon one another in fulfilling all the wants and needs to which we, as humans, are held subject.

While on the topic of interdependence, it may prove beneficial to consider the ideas of independence and codependence as well in an effort to provide a means of comparison in evaluating the relative benefit of each approach to interrelatedness. Independence connotes a lack of dependence or reliance on others. It speaks to the prospect of meetings one's own needs irrespective of fulfilling those of one's partner and, potentially, through different means than one's companion may have chosen. Consider, for example, my father's "rock-picking" adventures. However few and far between those excursions may have been, they served to promote my father's interests . . . *and his alone*. They did nothing but perturb my mother, as her ability to meet her own needs through independent means may have been somewhat limited in comparison with his. *It wasn't often that she took flight and left him home alone with the kids. However, she was an avid movie fan and reader of romance novels and managed to while away some hours on her own.* As I have mentioned, my father's singular pursuits seemed to diminish rather than enhance the degree of unity he was able to establish with my mother. Now that I think of it, so did hers.

Codependence has been a focus of therapeutic discussion in recent decades[31] and is seen as one individual's overly great reliance on another for meeting his or her needs to the point of enabling dysfunction on either or both parts. A common example would be the dependence of a substance addict on members of his or her family for temporal support while spending all his or her

---

[31] Beattie, M. (1987). *Codependent No More: How to Stop Controlling Others and Start Caring for Yourself.* New York, NY: Harper/Hazelden.

100

time, energy, and financial means engaged in the abuse. Oftentimes, an entire family system can be utilized in maintaining the addiction until dysfunctional patterns of interrelatedness are replaced with healthier ones. Codependence, therefore, does not connote a positive meaning.

While a certain amount of independence is required of each individual human being to function properly within our society, interdependence within a relationship serves as a means of drawing one closer to one's companion. My daughter has, at times, commented on how independent I used to be before pairing off with my spouse and has occasionally questioned me on my choices to wait to consult with him prior to making even small decisions or to hold off on meal preparation or shopping excursions until he can join me. That's my way of maintaining peace and harmony within our relationship and of including my partner in my life as fully as possible, as a large part of our time is spent apart in separate work endeavors. Now that my daughter has a husband of her own, she is coming to perceive things more from my perspective. *Why continue to stand alone in the world when there is a pair of arms to uphold you?* There is time enough for singular endeavors when your companion isn't around.

In considering some of your own observations and life experiences, what examples of interdependence in men's relationships with women come to mind? Again, those may include, but are not limited to, interactions between parents, grandparents, uncles and aunts, neighbors, and friends.

_____

_____

_____

_____

_____

_____

_____

_____

_How do you, as a man, apply interdependence in your life
and in your interactions with the women you know?_

_____

_____

_____

_____

_____

_____

_____

_____

In what ways do you perceive you might improve?

_____

_____

_____

_____

_____

_____

_____

How might those improvements enhance your life and your relationships?

_____

_____

_____

_____

_____

_____

_____

Establishing a mutually satisfying level of *interconnectedness* in one's union is a necessary element in enhancing its quality and duration. Degrees of *enmeshment* and *interdependence* both must be taken into account as he coordinates *his* efforts with *hers* in attaining that goal.

Chapter Six

"A Pound of Cure"

No relationship is free of problems, and a wise man fully invests in learning how to help resolve those, as he cannot always prevent them. Many influences, both surrounding and intrinsic to the relationship, may infiltrate his nest of love and disturb the relative tranquility which he has enjoyed. Finances, illness, family and work-related concerns all take their bite out of wedded bliss and leave little more than crumbs if man does not dissuade them. Also, failing to really talk with his lady or to share common views on togetherness may further injure their bond. Therefore, learning how to settle conflict before it gets out of hand is one means necessary in providing safety for his union, in buffering it from life's storms, and in lending longevity that leads to permanence, *but what exactly does that mean? Problem solving*[32] is a simple process which involves: 1) defining the problem, 2) brainstorming possible solutions, 3) considering the potential costs and benefits of applying each solution, 4) choosing a solution, 5) implementing a solution, and 6) evaluating the overall effectiveness of that solution. Implementing and evaluating the effectiveness of other solutions may be necessary should the original selection prove to be less than advantageous.

---

[32] Kendall, P. C. (1992). *Stop and Think Workbook.* Merion Station, PA: P. C. Kendall.

What does it mean to *define a problem?* Man must consider many things when attempting to understand all the facets involved in problem definition. First, *what* is the problem? Is it a behavior of concern on the part of one spouse or the other? Is it the way he or she may be thinking or feeling? Is it something from outside the relationship that may be interjecting its unholy presence into the sanctity of that holy union? It could be anything that causes worry for one or the other partner or both as they try to live peaceably with one another and in harmony with their surroundings. To illustrate, let's think back to the example of the wife who made an expensive purchase without consulting her husband. Especially from the husband's perspective, the problem would have been the expenditure and the lack of consultation beforehand, or, in other words, *his wife's behavior*, but *why* would she have taken such an action without consulting him? That leads us to the second part of problem definition, exploring *the underlying motivation.* In regard to the purchase, itself, the wife may have noted a need for bigger, newer appliances, as she, alone, was doing all the laundry in the household and felt somewhat imposed upon, especially in light of the fact that her old machines were not large enough and did not seem to be functioning properly. She may have thought her husband would be in disagreement with the purchase if she asked him about it, and, so, she took action on her own. She may or may not have been right about her husband's unwillingness to offer his consent, but we now have some insight into why she acted as she did. Some further elements that might be considered when defining a problem would include *who* is involved, *in this case, the wife, where* and *when* it occurs, *at the appliance store while her husband is working,* and *how*, or by what means, it is brought about, *with the assistance of the appliance store delivery truck and staff.*

Now that we have defined the problem in our illustration, what are some potential ideas to resolve it? At this point in the process, a man and a woman can allow their imaginations to run wild. They should *consider every possible solution that may be of help.* They mustn't ignore any of them because they never know what will work and do not want to disregard a suggestion that may prove to be beneficial. One answer to their quandary may be to return the appliances to the store with the agreement that the husband will aid the wife by helping with the laundry each week and that he will look into refurbishing the old machines so they will function more adequately. Another thought might be for the couple to keep the new machines with the understanding that other expenditures may have to be foregone within the household until the appliances are paid off. In addition, the husband and wife could work to overcome the poor communication patterns that contributed to the problem in the first place. The wife may agree to be more willing to share her concerns with her husband and to consult with him about how he can better help to meet her needs, and the husband might promise to try to be more open in his responses as his wife attempts to approach him.

The couple will now want to *consider the possible costs and benefits of applying each solution.* In regard to returning the new machines to the store and refurbishing the old ones, the couple decides that, while they will be saving some money overall, they will have to pay a restocking fee and the cost to repair the old appliances will be more than they are worth. Pertaining to lending a hand with the laundry, the husband realizes it will require some additional time and effort on his part. However, the benefits of showing his love and appreciation to his wife by offering to help her with some of the more mundane household tasks may be immeasurable. *Remember the jar of weeds?* In regard to keeping the new machines and foregoing other expenditures in the household, the couple realizes they might have to postpone a planned vacation until they are paid for or hold off on repairing a secondary vehicle for a time. While there will be some sacrifices involved, having the new appliances may prove worthwhile, as their efficiency will allow the wife more freedom for other pursuits. Finally, in respect to the communication issue, the couple agrees that learning how to talk to one another in sharing concerns may not be easy or readily forthcoming and that they might feel somewhat uncomfortable as they try something new in their relationship. However, they both anticipate the rewards in being more open with and accepting of each other.

After having weighed the costs and benefits of applying each solution, *a decision is made.* The couple will keep the new machines with the understanding that their budget will be somewhat limited for a time in regard to other expenditures. The husband agrees to help his wife with a number of laundry loads per week, and both husband and wife, realizing the dilemma their lack of good communication has caused, vow to try a little harder to be more open and accepting in discussing their thoughts and feelings, their wants and needs.

The solution is then implemented. It may take some weeks or even months to determine how effective it might be. One or the other spouse or both may falter in fulfilling their promises, thus, diminishing the power of their initial resolve. However, they have put the wheels of change into motion, and they can start them again if they come to a halt. Also, in this particular instance, as the couple will likely never have the opportunity to try the solution that was initially discarded, returning the new machines and refurbishing the old, they may never know how beneficial it might have been. However, in many problem-solving situations, *one solution can be more readily exchanged for another if the original choice proves to be disadvantageous.*

The previous example is what we might refer to as *problem solving in a nutshell*. It gives us a glimpse of what the process is all about and what it looks like to move from one step to another as *he* and *she* work together to find resolution to life's quandaries which they share in common. To further illustrate the concept, we might consider my parents' ongoing feud over my father's love for rocks and stretching his legs in the great outdoors and my mother's disdain for his occasional absences and lack of help with their mutual household responsibilities. According to my mother, not having my father's help, however infrequent and short in duration that may have been, was *what* constituted the problem. *Why* did he leave? It was because he loved having a little freedom and independence to do his own thing once in a while. *Who* was involved? It was my dad and his handful of "rock-picking" buddies. *When* and *where* did it happen? It only happened as often as Dad could get away with it, *and that wasn't very often*, but, when it did happen, it may very well have been in the same West Desert where my husband has also found enjoyment and temporary relief from life's many concerns. *How*, or by what means, did the offense take place? It was probably with very limited finances and usually with the aid of a vehicle that, more often than not, would break down in the middle of nowhere and leave Dad and his buddies stranded and having to walk great distances to reach civilization. *That was just part of the fun.*

Now that we've defined the problem, let's try to resolve it. What are some possible solutions that Mom and Dad could have generated in their heads to try to institute a little more peace in their home and in their hearts? For one thing, Dad could have decided just to forego ever venturing out on his own again. Under those circumstances, he would have stayed home and been completely miserable for the rest of his life. However, Mom probably would have been quite happy. On the other hand, Mom could have chosen to make peace with Dad's absence as well as good use of her time alone, with the kids, her extended family, or friends. She may not have liked having Dad gone but could, potentially, have endured it without experiencing quite as much trauma as his trips west usually engendered. That option likely would have met with Dad's approval. My parents could also have divorced. That might have lessened the contention between them. However, they decided early on in their relationship that was not a good idea. My oldest brother was born approximately 15 months after my parents were married, and they didn't want him to endure the hardships that may have accompanied a divorce. His six younger siblings were likewise blessed with a secure, *if not always harmonious*, home environment. What else could my parents have done to enhance their unity and lessen their bickering? Mom could have ventured out with Dad alone or have taken the whole crew along. Mom may not have appreciated nature quite like Dad did, but showing an interest in his enjoyments would likely have drawn them closer together. Also, while it may have been quite a production to include the kids, they, too, may have grown nearer to their father and more appreciative of his interests.

As you may have noticed, in the process of brainstorming possible solutions to my parents' dilemma, I also took the liberty to relay some potential costs and benefits of applying each one. That was done for the sake of brevity in considering my parents' situation and may be done in relation to your own problem-solving scenarios as long as you *make sure to fully exhaust the brainstorming process, ensure that no potential solution is discarded prematurely, and consider every possible cost and benefit associated with each one.* So, in regard to my parents' somewhat troubled relationship, they could have chosen a solution from the list above, tried it to see how well it worked to meet both their needs, and then explored other options if their first choice did not prove satisfactory.

In regard to what actually happened in my parents' relationship, Dad always retained his zest for fun and adventure, and Mom became more complacent in her role as wife and mother, even in Dad's absence, especially in light of her children's growing capabilities to meet their own needs as they matured with age. As I noted before, she had some singular endeavors of her own to turn to as well. Though time became the great healer in their particular circumstance, I pause to wonder how things might have been different if they had put forth the necessary effort to explore the possibilities that lay before them in choosing a joint path of healing early on in their relationship. How might that have impacted their lives and those of their children? I guess I'll never know for sure, and it probably doesn't matter so much in retrospect, but if they'd known then what I've come to learn about solving problems, I hope it would have made a difference for them. I hope it makes a difference for you, too. Now, it's up to you to fill in the details.

In considering some of your own observations and life experiences, what examples of problem solving in men's relationships with women come to mind? Again, those may include, but are not limited to, interactions between parents, grandparents, uncles and aunts, neighbors, and friends.

_____

_____

_____

_____

_____

_____

_____

_____

How do you, as a man, apply problem solving in your life and in your interactions with the women you know?

_____

_____

_____

_____

_____

_____

_____

_____

_____

In what ways do you perceive you might improve?

_____

_____

_____

_____

_____

_____

_____

How might those improvements enhance your life and your relationships?

_____

_____

_____

_____

_____

_____

_____

_____

_____

While "an ounce of prevention" can often eliminate the need for "a pound of cure," sometimes it's just too late to derail trouble from its destined course into our lives and our love relations. When that is the case, active, mutual engagement in problem solving is a tool for building unity between a man and a woman. The solution, itself, is secondary to the process from which it evolves. As a couple coordinates their efforts in learning to overcome one dilemma, they gain the ability to conquer most, if not all, problematic circumstances that life may bring their way. As the old adage goes,

Give a man a solution to a problem, and he celebrates the day.
Teach him how to solve his own problems, and the days of his celebration may be never ending.

Conclusion

Much has been written by way of admonishment and instruction in the pages of this book, and much is to be gained by the reader if he will fully apply what he has learned. The intent has been to raise his aspirations as to what he might attain in the way of love relations with his female counterpart. "To have and to hold"[33] are words precious to hear that might be lifted as standard for one whose heart is truly invested in loving another forever in time. To win a woman's love and acceptance and commune with her as one are needs most basic in man's pursuit. Then, he must arm himself with attributes necessary to enhance longevity and permanence in his union. In addition, he is obliged to march beside his lady to the beat of a common drummer as they search for a degree of interconnectedness which meets both their needs. Finally, he cannot help but enlist her aid in battling life's foes as they, together, seek to conquer all problems which come their way. Those are means most principle in carrying man forth to journey's end, where life, however short or long, and years, be they many or few, are made

---

[33] That quotation is taken from the *Book of Common Prayer*, compiled under the direction of Thomas Cranmer (1489-1556), Archbishop of Canterbury under Henry VIII and Edward VI, and first printed in 1549 though having undergone many revisions since that time. An earlier reference to the quotation "to habben and to holden" is that of *Piers the Plowman* (1362), attributed to the English poet, William Langland. His birth and death years are unknown.

rich and full of light when spent beside the woman of his dreams, "the apple of his eye,"[34] his lady love.

---

[34] "something, or more usually someone, cherished above others" – "The phrase is exceedingly old and first appears in Old English in a work attributed to King Aelfred (the Great) of Wessex, AD 885, entitled *Gregory's Pastoral Care*. The earliest recorded use in modern English is in Sir Walter Scott's *Old Mortality*, 1816: 'Poor Richard was to me as an eldest son, the apple of my eye.'" – as cited on www.phrases.org.uk/meanings